WHY MEN RUN

away...

Cedella Blanchard

To my husband,
who believed in me even when I did not.
I love you

Copyright page

This first edition is edited, designed and published by
FinalDraft Editing & Publishing Services, Mississauga, Canada, 2021

Editing team: Priti Raghavan (Singapore), Kaberi Dutta Chatterjee (Canada)

Designer: Cover page, back cover and spine: Anirban Paul (India), Aneesh Chatterjee (Canada)

Formatting, book designing for publication: Kaberi Dutta Chatterjee

(Website: https://www.facebook.com/finaldraftofnovels)

ISBN: 978-0-9920784-7-8

Paperback printed by Amazon.com, USA, for USA, UK, Canada, Italy, Spain, Germany, France, Japan, Australia

eBook distributed globally by Amazon

Author Photograph: Selfie by author

We are seriously flawed.
The things that are the most necessary, the most critical
to us, are the things we take most for granted.
Air. Water. Love.

If you have someone to love, you are lucky.
If they love you back, you're blessed.
And if you waste the time you have to love them,
you're a fool

~*Richard Paul Evans*

CONTENTS

PREFACE

Everything you need to know about

love and relationships

ONE THING that always perplexes me is to see two people who were once madly in love becoming distant strangers. Strangers, who can hardly bear the sight of each other. It breaks my heart to even think that something that was once so beautiful, couples who had loved one another, made plans, promises, commitments and vows, broke it all in the end.

In many instances, the situation could have been handled differently and easily fixed, if only they had taken the time to talk it over.

We all agree that men and women are on two different spectrums in life, which causes us to view things through different lenses at times. However, communicating and discussing issues before they are escalated could help save many of those failed relationships.

For many of us growing up as young girls, it was our dream to meet our perfect prince and marry him one day. Though, we may not have fully conceptualized the complete dynamics of what a relationship or even a marriage entailed, we dreamt of it. We hoped our love stories would end like those teenage love story movies that we saw.

Stepping into adulthood, I learned quickly that relationships are anything but the ones in the fairy tale movies and books. It is amazing to find how much time people spend thinking about relationships, and it always appears as though they spend an even greater time trying to fix them. One thing I have learned over the years, is that men and women speak two completely different languages and because of this, the relationships have suffered immensely.

As women, we have compromised so much for our men and yet it has landed us little to nowhere. Many of us have sacrificed education, friends, families and careers to be with the man we loved, only to end up feeling hurt and betrayed in the end.

One thing I have distinctly observed is that in majority of the cases, women always tend to get the blame. A man can go out and do whatever he wants, victimise a woman completely, but somehow the fingers are more often than not pointed at her — that she wasn't good enough, or she didn't treat him well.

In this book, my aim is to share things that I've observed over the years about family, friends and acquaintances. I will give valuable insights which I believe would help to improve and educate not just women, but men too, in what it means to have a lasting and meaningful relationship.

The goal, however, is to help make women stronger and feel empowered about themselves.

To ensure that women believe they are more than enough. To enable women to look at things from different perspectives about the choices they make before taking life-changing decisions.

Have you ever met up with your girlfriends for a night out and all you could talk about was your man and how they have wronged you? Sometimes, I even joke around saying that it is the season for failed relationships. Women always seem to put in the most in their relationships. We always tend to reciprocate little to no love from our men with an abundance of it. This is something that has always mystified me and has led to my questioning many things. Why is it that we can never get the love we desperately need and deserve? Is it that men are so egotistic and engulfed with their own desires that they honestly cannot see how much hurt and pain they cause? Or is it that societal norms have programmed our thinking so much that they believe it is weakness for a man to show sensitivity to the woman he supposedly loves?

Whatever the questions and whatever the answers, I will try my best to resolve them here. I assure you there will be no bias against men and how they may be the ones who are always at fault. The book is also intended to shed light on things we as women might be doing to hurt our own relationships. After all, it does take two to tango, and I am fully aware of how spiteful some women can become when things are not going their way.

Even so, many of us tend to lose our true self in becoming what we think a man needs of us by diminishing ourselves, our beliefs and our values.

I often sit and worry at times, not for myself but for the three girls I am a mother to. I worry because I do not want to see any of them growing up to experience the hurt and pain caused by someone they love. I also worry for my son because I never want him to impose those pain and hurt on anyone.

I wish that my girls do not grow up expecting a fairy-tale life which doesn't exist. I know they will want all the things most women desire in life one day. A loving, supportive husband, with whom they can fulfill life and build a family. I owe it to them and also to the millions of women who suffer (some silently) every day in their relationships. I also hope that our men will read this and see how much pain they cause us. We sincerely ask for nothing more than just to be loved the same way that we love them.

PART 1

Understanding that life is not a fairy tale

IMAGINE yourself looking out from an airplane window. The captivating view from way up there serves as an illustration of the perfect life you want to live. The calming overview of blue and green, dark and light divided into stately and majestic mountains and the never-ending ocean bowing at their feet. The radiant sunshine kissing the face of the crystal waters. The world seems still, and the panorama gives you a sense of tranquillity, a feeling of love and of nonchalance which diminishes all fears and worries in your life. And for that moment, you feel at peace.

I was 12 years old when my elder sister got married to who seemed at the time her perfect Mr Right. I remember the joy I felt watching them getting married and how wonderful it all seemed. At that tender age, I thought love would be everything you ever wanted and that after marriage you would live the life you read about in fairy tales. I looked at them and pictured a life that would be as perfect as they seemed. A few years later, my sister and her husband were divorced. Fast forward 14 years, again was she from her second husband. I realized that life isn't a fantasy and love isn't all that easy as we tend to believe. It was hard for me to fathom how something so beautiful could have ended so badly and I could not help but question the reasons as to why people fall out of love. Have you ever wondered why in a fantasy story they never show their lives after the princess finds her perfect prince? Because that is when the real story begins.

When I became an adult and started dating, I began to understand the depths, the ups and downs of relationships. I met and fell in love with my first boyfriend in my late teens. Though things never really started out quite as seriously until I reached my 20s, I shared an amazing 14 years of my life with him and never conceptualized that one day it would come to an end. But it did!

Relationships were never quite the same after that and I quickly learned that fairy-tale romances were just that.

Fairy tales!

There is much more to having a serious relationship with a partner than them just having a cute face, or excessive hormones. The hormones just create a sense of dependency and a feeling of want. Most women still live in that fantasy and do not realize that we need to move away from those childish expectations about relationships. In the psychological essence of love, when teenagers fall in love, it is a whole new experience, never yet faced. Their brains and bodies undergo a change never yet encountered and therefore, a dependable need of emotion increases, along with the desires of love and attention. This is the first stage of love (which I will discuss in detail later). Unlike teenage relationships, the older we get, our relationships become more about 'intention' and not just 'attention'. There is a purpose and an aim to achieve something in life and having someone to do it with. You learn to grow from your failures and help to build each other up.

Hence, in other words, it is moving from a state of the physical, to something more in-depth. It is securing a solid future with a person you have a desire of journeying through life with.

When we think of the phrase 'Mr Right', we often conjure an image of someone tall, dark and handsome, who will be there to fulfill our every need. Or, even this perfect prince, who would one day come, sweep us off our feet and ride away into the sunset, where we would live happily ever after. These portrayals are appealing and may have been instilled in us from a young age by fantasy stories and teenage romance movies.

Most of us grow up believing that such melodramatic love really does exist. A picture-perfect love, without failures or flaws! Owing to this fantasy, many of us enter relationships with the overly-exaggerated expectation of perfection and are unprepared when we discover some flaws. We fail to see that it is within those moments of imperfection that the true love story emerges. Don't get me wrong though, I'm sure there are people who have found their perfect prince, their very own Mr Right. I am equally sure they too come with their own flaws which, at times, have led to bitter disagreements. Some, on the other hand, may have found Mr Right, but drove him away as they lacked the awareness that they were supposed to move through different stages of love. Thus, the title 'Why Men Run, away'.

So, what is it in a man that makes us feel he is the "right one"? And when we find him, how do we keep him from running away? Or even know that he is the 'one'?

First off, we must get into the mindset that we are different people. There are things your other half will enjoy doing that you don't, and vice versa. That is alright! If we found someone who was exactly like us, how boring would that be! It is the differences in opinion, that I think, strengthens the relationship. It is the best way to challenge each other's feelings and views in a constructive way.

Unfortunately, many of us are not good at arguing and as a result, situations like this serve as a catalyst that start vitriolic arguments. It is our duty, if it's our aim to be supportive partners, wishing to build lasting unions, to learn how to handle situations like these, if and when they do present themselves.

An example of this could be a talk with your husband about starting a family. He may think both of you are not ready financially, but you, however, have a different viewpoint and insist that it is time. An argument ensues, hurtful and bitter words are exchanged. This compromises a situation that increases the risk of losing each other. You may get all emotional, run off crying, leaving the situation unaddressed, causing tension for weeks. And in extreme cases, can even cause the termination of the relationship.

In most circumstances, since the situation was not dealt with properly, every time any other argument develops, the topic is broached upon and there is no real closure. This gradually builds, turning the matter into a state much harder to handle. When conditions like these do arise, it is best to sit and talk to each other. Discussing each of your expectations, trying to make a compromise and meeting each other halfway.

Maybe, he thinks you are not financially ready, and you think no one is really financially prepared for a family. Maybe, instead of being upset with him, suggesting that you both open an investment account within a certain period would allow you to start a family. He, too, should understand that a woman's body works on a biological clock and that there may not be an indefinite amount of time to wait. It is essential that each person's views are put across in a respectful manner. Only then will there be an option of how to move forward. This is one way of finding solutions for concerns.

Many couples avoid confrontations, but one should acknowledge that there is absolutely nothing wrong with having an argument. It all depends on the way one argues. Jonathan Safran Foer once said, "You cannot protect yourself from sadness without protecting yourself from happiness." It is inevitable that you will get hurt and be dismayed, especially in the pursuit of happiness. You cannot encounter joy without having to undergo grief. It is a natural cycle to life.

Applying practicality, learning effective communication and being open to the good, the bad, and the indifference are necessary steps you need to take with your partner to show that you are willing and accepting of him and whatever life throws at you. Addressing issues as they happen and not excessively prolonging them is the cue to a strong relationship. Some of us end up living in misery due to a fairy tale expectation we've developed and wait forever to find the perfect guy, when in all possibilities, most of the times, he is right there. Due to our ignorance and fictional anticipations, we push him away.

By no means are men exempt from this. It is a two-way street.

Mr Right shouldn't be about how good-looking your man is, or how much money he has in his bank account, though in all fairness, those would be added bonuses. The Mr Right I have in mind, is the one who is there for you emotionally, physically and spiritually. Someone, you will be able to build a future with. Someone, who is compatible with you.

It's funny how most people spend a great amount of time searching for the ideal partner, and when they do find them, they spend their time trying to change them. With divorce and separation rates at an all-time high, I think it is time we started looking at relationships from a different perspective.

We must try to understand that no relationship is perfect. A truly wonderful relationship is about the imperfections, the candid moments you get to share with your loved one. This helps the relationship to grow and, in my opinion, adds flair and character. Whatever you use to win a person over, should be what you use to keep them. So, if you were the ultimate angel at the beginning of the relationship and a year later you turn out to be a witch, then that is just a selfish act of manipulating people to believing you were something that you are not. You must remain consistent and true to who you are.

To make a relationship successful there are certain principles you should adhere to. It is like the definitive blueprint to a happy and successful relationship. A union cannot be very successful without:

COMMUNICATION

Effective communication is imperative in building and maintaining a happy and healthy relationship. In fact, it is the forming foundation to the other fundamentals. It is much more than discussions about bills, the kids or what movie to watch. It is about being able to convey your hopes, aspirations, dreams and fears.

Relationships are investments and they require a lot of hard work. You will also need to accept the fact that not every day or everything will go smoothly or in the way you planned it. Yet, by learning to talk to your partner about how you feel, you will get to structure a firm foundation that will encourage effective communication.

It is also important to discuss topics of sensitive nature in-person. You give each other a chance to say how you both feel and get the opportunity to read each others' reactions. It is important to avoid discussing serious matters by just texting. Written messages can easily be misinterpreted, which may lead to even bigger problems fostering.

It is important that you be supportive of each others' needs, take the time to listen to each other and evaluate things carefully before responding. You should also be careful with your body language. You don't want to give your partner the impression that you're not interested in what they're saying or that your point is the only one that is valid. Be each other's main support.

After a long day at work, you should be able to come home and feel a sense of peace with each other. Be the comfort zone that the other longs for. I get very excited about finally going home at the end of the day to see my man. Seeing him relieves me of all the day's stress.

Be transparent and honest in your relationship, never be afraid to tell each other how you feel about any situation. We often shove sensitive issues under the rug in the hope of avoiding a heated argument, when in truth not addressing the situation will lead to a serious miscommunication.

We tend to link arguments with quarrels and bad outcomes, but arguments should be used as a platform of good reasoning where both are able to reach harmonious compromise.

There are three possible outcomes of an argument. We can choose to leave it alone and nothing will be resolved, we can get into it and it turns out poorly, or we can face it and deal with it maturely. Given the choices, I would personally go for the third option. Sometimes, we leave issues unaddressed, and in the future when something else comes up, everything unravels, issues that are not even relevant at that moment are dredged up. Arguing about the same things over and over will never help your relationship to heal. Therefore, end an argument with an acceptable solution. It's kind of like "Never go to bed angry". Same concept. Never leave an argument unsolved.

TIME

Relationships are investments. A relationship has never and will never work without giving it your time. If a long-lasting relationship is what you seek, then quality time together will be needed. So many people are guilty of forming a better bond with someone other than their spouse, but the relationship with your partner should be the one most embraced and profound. As a result, it requires a lot more of your time and effort.

Many relationships are broken due to not investing and spending time with each other. You cannot agree to love someone, then turn around and be committed only to yourself. When you reach a decision of starting a union with someone, you will need to learn to include the other in your hopes and dreams, to live life together, to value each other and to treat each other with abundant attention and care. It is learning to invest quality time daily. To acquire a meaningful relationship is more valuable than any momentary or temporary thing that one chases. It is a beautiful feeling when you love and care for another person who is there to share everything with you for a lifetime.

TRUST

Trust is the basis of any relationship. If you don't trust your partner, in all probability, you should end your relationship. It seems that most women are guilty of this trait. Not that men are not, but women tend to show more insecurities than men. Women tend to behave unpredictably when they get suspicious about their men. They go through their partners' belongings to see what they could have been up to. Such actions trigger an unhealthy relationships. You really don't need to know what your man is doing all the time; you don't need to follow your man around or popup unannounced just to see what he's been up to.

If you have reasons to believe that your partner is unfaithful, most likely he is (and I am talking about situations where the evidence is conspicuous. I am not referring to crazy insecurities). Your intuition works with your subconscious and prompts you when things are off and seem unnatural. The greatest advice I could give you is end it and move on.

Now, there are other women who would go through all the trouble of finding this out only to hurt themselves by taking no action. If you aren't going to leave or do anything about the situation, then let it go! You have already subjugated to accepting sharing him.

Sometimes, we have some real good men in our lives, but it's just the crazy things we do that drives them away. Constantly nagging your man about things like cheating, based on suspicions will get him thinking about it and eventually push him to do so, even if he was initially honest and true.

RESPECT

People have different connotations of the term 'respect'. Often, it is shown to people in authoritative positions and would therefore imply that only people with a certain type of power or stature should be respected. However, it is significant to remember the fundamentals of life and understand that we should treat others in ways we would like to be treated. In a relationship, one must understand that no one has any authority over the other.

We surely are different individuals with varied views and interests. However, if you go out of your way to value your partner and his feelings, it can become a fundamental building block in the relationship. Your partner should, and will have a different opinion, which may be different than yours. The key to the story is acceptance! The more you accept and give respect, the more you'll get it. Respect is earned, and to get it, you'll have to give it. Arguments are a healthy part of relationships, but you must learn to find a common ground when you disagree on something. To be able to respect others, you must first be able to respect yourself. Respecting yourself is not saying that the world revolves around you. It means that you are comfortable in your skin. You regard yourself in high value. As such, you know how to regard others. By honoring your partner, you can put yourself completely at peace.

FAITH

In Hebrews 11:6 it tells us that without faith it is impossible to please God. Likewise, without faith in your relationship, it is impossible to have a good relationship. Having faith requires belief; believing that whatever life throws at you, that you will be able to work it out and overcome the challenging situations together. Faith is not something one can touch or feel, it is something like hope and love. You open your heart and give it a chance with the trust that it will work. When you let someone in your life, you are letting down your guard and opening the door to your soul to this person. Faith gives you that mettle to move forward and the belief that the journey is worth it. For a lasting relationship, one has to have faith in oneself and the partner.

When couples believe in each other and start to see their relationship as a place of comfort and growth, it makes it easier to share new ideas and get each others' opinions. This promotes a healthy, fun and loving environment for both. Therefore, having faith is one of the fundamentals to a lasting union.

PART 2

THE LOVE CYCLE

Living in an era where our lives are almost completely graphed by gadgets and social media, we cannot help but notice other seemingly perfect couples who often popup on our social timelines. As much as we hate to admit it, very often the skeptic in us kicks in when we see this. And we begin to question the genuineness of their relationships. How long will they last, we might want to ask? Are they really that happy? How come they always seem to be so lovey-dovey?

That being said, we must understand that life is not a perfect bubble, that we have tides. Taking a practical approach is the key.

An honest and open relationship is prudent to its survival. It is noteworthy that nothing lasts forever, and all things, good or bad, do come to an end. In relationships, the end might be through separation or death.

One would bend backwards to make their relationship work, but it is not worth subjugating and humiliating oneself in an unhealthy/unhappy relationship.

It may be mature to acknowledge the fact that it might not last, but not to dwell on it. You may want to enjoy every moment that you get to spend with each other to create beautiful memories.

Growing up in a Christian family, we were taught that successful marriages are highly contingent in their length. Someone might ask a married couple, "How long have you been married?"

The success of a relationship should not be based on its length, but rather its merits. Lengthy relationships can also be as unsuccessful as short-lived ones. If you asked your mother or grandmother what made their relationship successful, they may say 'God', but we know that it is not entirely true. In all probability, they may have hung onto their relationships praying to God everyday to make it right. And at the end of their days, when neither could move about much or protest much, they lived depending on each other and called it a successful marriage.

However, there is no guarantee that a relationship will last forever. Or even if it does, that it lasted for the right reasons. Our emotions are unpredictable, and love does not come with a manual.

Being with someone is a lot of hard work. We often think that love is enough to keep him. No, it is not. Every wedding which I have attended, including my own, newlyweds are compared to couples who have been married for an extensive number of years. They tell us to strive to be like those with lengthy relationships.

We often honor those achievers celebrating milestones of 10, 20, 30, 40 and even 50 years. But is that enough?

Before I got married, I thought that getting married was enough, all the rest would come easy. Boy, was I wrong! After I got married, I started learning things about my husband I did not know. I am sure the same applied to him about me.

There is a popular saying in my native Jamaica, *"Si mi an cum live with mi a two different thing".* It means appearances can be deceptive. This enhances the fact that to date someone with whom you have never lived, is completely different from actually living with that person.

Living with someone is difficult, especially during the first year, as this is when you really learn of a person's true oddity. So, to say years of relationship is equivalent to a successful one, is like comparing yourself to a lazy employee who thinks promotions or raises should be given based on years of service and not quality of work.

Successful relationships should be appraised by how one feels after years of being together. "Do I still love him?" "Can we hold a good conversation without wanting to kill each other?" "Am I happy?"

There are so many couples out there who are stuck in despondent relationships and have become comfortable with just co-existing. Some might say we are doing it for the kids, or simply because it is more economical. There are those that are just forcing themselves to rake up the years without the relationship having any true substance. Very often, it is done out of fear of what others might say. I, personally, would much rather have a delightful short-lived relationship than one of just co-existence.

Love is a cycle and sometimes we exhaust all the phases of love in our relationship, causing it to end. A successful relationship acknowledges the fact that an end is a possibility. When this happens, a lot of us live our lives in regret and disillusionment.

I do not think things happen to us in life by chance, and therefore a failed relationship should not be equated as a waste. Instead, it should be looked upon as a enrichment to our soul. That we know how to love!

After a failed relationship, one should be able to look back and know that you have contributed to making each other better, having shared life. If your relationship comes to an end, you should leave knowing you were changed for the better. You gained strength and have been shaped into a more resilient version of yourself. Most importantly, leave with zero regrets.

Relationships are about learning to love someone behind the scenes- the real person. It is learning to love that person even when you hit a wall, by finding a way to go over it, under it, around it or just breaking through it. It is about learning to make compromises. It is accommodating the fact that he might never be into the same things as you are in and it is acceptable to you. It is acknowledging that looking for flawlessness in him is a definite way to set yourself up for disappointment. It is being able to understand that changes are inevitable.

Based on the title of the book, you might say that I am contradicting myself by telling you that there is a cycle of love, and if so, how can we call back Mr Right if the love cycle has ended. Finding your Mr Right and stopping him from running away is not necessarily going back to the past form of love.

My intention is to guide you through a successful relationship and propose some of the things one can do to make it a lasting one. This is to help you identify areas where you might have gone wrong in a past relationship and assist you in making better choices in the future.

At times, we cause our relationships to end prematurely and by acknowledging our mistakes, we could help in making the existing one a little more meaningful, or by just becoming more prepared.

After years of observing others and from my own experiences, I've come to the realization that to sincerely enjoy a relationship is to accept that relationships are not a state of interminable ecstasy.

As women and even more so as human beings, we undergo different states of emotions: fear, jealousy, anger, sadness, pride among many others. These are felt during many circumstances of the relation and cannot be overlooked.

Truth be told, relationships will amplify these feelings. A person's flaws become more evident when you become intimate.

You cannot help but feel a hint of jealousy when another woman hugs your man too closely or a sense of discomfort when you walk past a notably attractive woman, and he is peering over his shoulders. This is just the nature of life. But if you think about things rationally, you will probably realize that it is alright. He might just appreciate another woman's beauty just as we do in other men.

My husband will probably tell you that I do not have an ounce of jealousy in me, though that is a long way from the truth. I just choose not to make an issue out of that minute thing. There will be other women he is attracted to, it is human nature, and I have learned to accept that. His response to this attraction and what he does in moments like these is an entirely different topic. However, if he acts out on his feelings, takes these temporary feelings of attraction seriously and puts his serious relationship at stake, it is a matter of concern.

Ultimately, your actions should not just be based on having a man and being in a relationship. It should be about enjoying each other and growing as you go along. Whether your relationship lasts for a week, a year, five years or a lifetime should not matter. What should matter is making each day count.

I feel it is important to avoid colourful expectations from each other and learn to live in the moment. Building a credible reality of the things one want from one another and working with that is more interesting.

PART 3

UNDERSTANDING YOUR
ROLE AS A WOMAN

As A young girl, I always wanted to become a doctor. I wanted to get married, yes, but I had never really put a great deal of thought into it. Though I knew I wanted a partner who would be great and treated me with respect, I also knew I wanted more out of a relationship than just the idea of being in one. I never really liked the idea of taking orders from a man just because he has manhood. I wanted to be able to throw just as much weight and contribute to my household as he does. I worried about finding a partner who would share my 'out of the norm' beliefs. Due to this, I became content with the possibility that I may never find him. I was fully prepared to go ahead with life on my own.

Kids were always a big deal for me. I always wished to have two kids. I would often imagine the joy motherhood would bring, but not necessarily having to be in a committed relationship to have them. Maybe, artificial insemination?

Today, I am a wife to an amazing husband, a biological mother to a beautiful baby girl and three wonderful stepchildren. They bring more joy to my life than I could have ever hoped for. Having obtained such a blissful family, I cannot help but get overly excited about wanting more. As for my career, well, I am currently working in pharmaceuticals. I started my pre-medical degree, which I never quite completed. I chose a path in psychology instead. I will, however, pursue my medical degree one day, I'm sure. My husband insists on it. Sometimes, when we make plans for the future, they never really turn out the way we hoped. I was blessed to find a husband who pushes me to do more and pursue my goals. For that I will be eternally grateful.

For centuries, women have been told that their role is to take care of the family and the house and that a man should be the breadwinner and provide for his family. I have a problem with limiting a woman to being domesticated. What if we want to step out and pursue our dreams and aspirations? In a committed relationship, you are making the promise to have each other's backs. That is how it should be in everything. Pick up the slack when the other falters.

PART 4

ON BECOMING
AND BEING A WIFE

I HAVE always been hesitant when it comes to talking about relationships and marriages with older people. Our culture, over centuries, has taught us that a woman's role is to always be submissive to her husband and the choices he makes. It had been instilled in us that a woman should always put the happiness of her children and her husband above her own. I've seen women dismiss their dreams so often, as they take on the role of being a wife. I find it appalling. What if my ideas and decisions are better than his? Maybe these dismal doctrines were reasons that made one so cautious about becoming someone's wife.

I met my husband about 10 years before we started dating. We became very close friends and over time, he developed an interest in me, which I admit, I did not share at the time. For starters, we had an 11-year age gap and he had already established a life which I had only hopes of starting. There was no denying though, that he had an amazing personality and a heart of gold. He never lost hope that one day we would be together. He would always tell me that I was his angel, I just did not know it then. Boy, was he right! He wasn't just a hopeless romantic though.

After getting to know him better, I was pleased to find out that he had no interest in dating a submissive woman. According to him, the greatest quality a woman could possess was of strength and the ability to challenge herself. He epitomizes the meaning of support and would encourage me (and continues to do so) to pursue my dreams and aspirations. He is the 'think it and he makes it happen' kind of guy.

My husband taught me that the only limits to life are those that we put ourselves. I watched him as a single father, who would go to the ends of the earth to make sure his children had a great life. If I know anything about love and relationships, I know that having someone, who always has your back, is someone worth keeping. Over time, I fell madly in-love with him, we started dating and the rest… Well, you know.

When you begin understanding yourself and your values, you will know the qualities you want in a man. Like me, you may not see his true potential at the time, but his attitude towards life will somewhat illustrate his sense of direction and where he is going. It would be evident if he is someone serious and committed. My husband saw that in me before I was even able to identify it in myself.

PART 5

THE FIVE STAGES OF LOVE

L IKE A love cycle, so too, there are different stages of love. While I was writing this chapter, I sat in an airplane observing the passengers take their seats. I could not help but notice the couples with overly insecure women. These women sprung into defense mode as soon as their man caught sight of another woman. Though, it was somewhat amusing to watch, I must say that experiencing sadness is as important as experiencing happiness.

It's human nature to shy away from things we find frustrating and difficult to deal with, but one cannot truly experience the beauty of life without experiencing the ugly sides too. Sometimes, we need to face the difficult parts of life in order to appreciate the meaningful side more when they occur.

Every noteworthy relationship starts in the same way. We meet someone, become attracted to them, go out on dates, go on a few more dates, get married, have kids, yeah, you got it. But through all of that, there are stages your love will go through whether you like it or not. Finding and identifying what stage you are in within your love cycle could help break through barriers and advance to the next level, while avoiding any awkwardness. It is also as important to know your partner's love stage and work with him through it since no two people are exactly the same.

STAGE ONE: THE MEET

A lot of people may describe the actions as obsession. He is perfect and without flaws in your eyes. Your heart beats pitter-patter whenever you see him, and it is as if the heavens shine a special light over him. Dopamine (the feel-good hormone which is also associated with addiction) is released in the brain and you become high from falling in-love. There is absolutely nothing he could do that would make you think otherwise. You want to spend every chance, every minute that you get with him. You catch yourself thinking about him all the time and he is completely irresistible to you.

Psychologists state that this stage of love is a period which helps in the selection process of finding the ideal mate. However, over time this need of love and want will change to companionship and bonding.

It is believed that during this time, your emotions help you fall in love. So, in other words, this is indeed an obsessive, infatuated state, and not necessarily true love. The first stage of love is normally very short lived, but one most people expect never to change.

STAGE TWO: FALLING IN LOVE

This is when you and the person you have fallen in love with decide to take things a bit further and commit to each other. It is where you will probably move in with him or where you both decide to get married. Like the first stage, this stage too, consists of high emotions and attractions. However, during this phase, you will begin to see your partner for who he really is and what he is really made of. The honeymoon bliss will wear off and you will start to notice his flaws. At the same time, you will start to see his true personality, his interests, likes and dislikes and get a glimpse of his true intentions towards you and the relationship.

Take into consideration though, that during this phase, he is also learning about you. Your compatibility will now be put to the ultimate test. It is obligatory that you know how to identify and act during this stage, as this will undoubtedly determine the outcome of your relationship.

At this point, you should be able to identify your man's style of loving and what type of a lover he is. It will probably be required of you to adjust your style of loving to accommodate his, and vice-versa. If not, you will have to decide if the relationship is worth pursuing. A lot of women will be quick to decide that they will not change for him. Sadly, I used to be that way too. This mindset leads to failure of the relationship.

No one is asking you to change your personality. Very often when we hear this, we misinterpret it into thinking he is trying to change me. You will never find a person who is exactly like you. We are all unique in our own right and have different interests in life. I would like to give you a personal example about when I just started dating my boyfriend of the time and who is now my husband. I really love to talk... A lot! My husband on the other hand is very observant. He likes to observe things well before passing judgment and making comments. In the beginning, I found this extremely challenging, and would often think that he has lost interest and has grown tired of me. Over time, I realized that was just how he is and though it took me awhile to understand him, I respected his ways and adjusted to accommodate him. I did not change myself, I still love to talk, but I know not to pester him for an immediate answer. I give him the time to assess the situation in order to divulge better suggestions.

When you learn to respect your partner, it also benefits you. He will see how much you respect him, and he will be placed in a position where he cannot help but appreciate you for accepting who he is. He will know that he will never find someone else with that quality and will treat you well.

STAGE THREE: THE TURNING POINT

This comes right after the committing stage and can creep up on you just when you start thinking you have made it, and everything is going well. This is the stage where many relationships actually sink. You begin to question what went wrong and how did you get here? You start to think that something is very wrong but in truth all meaningful relationships end up in this stage. Though love emits a lot of feel-good hormones throughout our bodies, it is also associated with us acting in irrational and eccentric ways.

Jealousy, anger and insecurities are emotions which accompany love. Negative outcomes may transpire as a result. We are familiar with the saying, "Too much of a good thing can also be bad for you." The same applies in the case of love. Always remember that there is a thin line between love and hate. Studies have shown that over-loving someone can have the same erratic consequences as a person suffering from addiction and has the same ability to impair one's cognition.

We often see this in women and men alike, who think that once they are romantically involved with someone, they have the right to control the person's thoughts and actions. These stem from a major trust breakdown in the relationship and can lead to the person becoming annoyed, driving the other to junctures of becoming adulterous or in extreme cases abusive. This could last days, months or even years and could most likely continue until something changes or the relationship has run its course.

STAGE FOUR: THE TRUE LOVE

A couple's authenticated love for each other is revealed during this stage. You have experienced the highs and lows of your relationship, learnt about each other, seen your partner at his worst, learned to resolve issues and have mastered the laws of effective communication. This is the rebirth of love where the old spark you once had will begin to re-emerge. You will start to feel a sense of fulfillment and triumph and it will seem as though you could conquer anything together.

This stage of love is mostly witnessed in your parents and grandparents' relationships. For most couples, this involves years of sacrifice. You now understand each other, and it seems as if you are completely in sync with the other. It is very rare that couples who get to this stage separate.

Let me point out something very important though. Movement through stages of a relationship is not accomplished completely by years of being together, it relies on how you work through the challenges. It is possible that people who are together for decades are stuck in a phase they are never able to move on from. To glide through each phase of love you need to truly understand each other and your different ways of love.

STAGE FIVE: THE HAPPILY EVER AFTER

Congratulations! You have now accomplished all that you had set out to and now it is time to sit back, relax and enjoy the fruits of your labour. You have gained a lifelong companion. This is the death do us part stage. You know him, he knows you. You know how to have constructive arguments without offending the other. You have now built a life where living without the other is somewhat hard and impossible.

WHAT REALLY MATTERS IN THE END

You will go through the different stages of love which will test every ounce of your love, loyalty, and commitment to your partner. What it all boils down to at the end of the day is the decision you both make to remain committed to each other. This will be your epicenter as you learn that feelings come and go, but what ties you forever is the commitments you make. The commitment to be faithful to your spouse even when the tides are low and through the hard trials of life make the core of a healthy relationship.

PART 6

BECOME MRS RIGHT

THE MINUTE you become seriously involved with someone, you want to know if the person is right for you. Is this your Mr Right? You might ask yourself, but are you someone's Ms/Mrs Right? Finding the right person can sometimes be tough. At first glance, you may love everything you see, then further down the road everything changes. To attract the right people in your life, you will need to possess the same qualities you seek in another. Be mindful of the fact that Mr Right is also analyzing you.

FINDING YOURSELF

Who are you? What are you searching for? Perhaps these are the most mind-boggling questions you have ever tried to answer about yourself. Your opinion about yourself is highly contingent on how others view you, your genetic makeup, life experiences and upbringing. Because a lot of behaviours are learned, it's easy for one's true self to be obscured. Someone may describe you as a very nice and polite person, who always smiles and treats people with respect, because that's the way you were taught to be, while deep inside, you may be depressed and do not like interacting with others.

Your personality should not depend entirely on how others view you, but what you know and think about yourself. Your true self is about your own unique characteristics and internal feelings. Finding who you truly are will help to prevent pretentious behaviours, in acceptance of your flaws and eventually working on fixing them. To attract Mr Right in your life and develop a healthy relationship, you need to first become Ms Right, by knowing exactly what it is you need.

On my quest to finding my Mr Right, I was taken on a spiritual journey to discover who I was. I learned to accept my flaws, challenged my fears and let go of my demons. I had to shed layers of my life, let go the negative aspects and learnt to grow. I moved away from the things that were not contributing positively to my life, and, as a result, I had to give up some family and friends. Moving away from them did not mean I did not love and appreciate them, but I learned to do so from a distance.

It is important to note that because someone may be related to you by blood, they should not be granted access to your life and how you should live it. Sometimes tolerating other's mediocrity may accentuate the mediocrity within yourself. Associating yourself with positive-minded people, will allow yourself to become like those you closely relate to. I allowed a higher power within me, so I was able to let my true soul shine. It takes hard work to find yourself and live a happy life. It's a process you work on developing and when you find your happiness, you should be able to make it into a practice.

PART 7

SELF-CREATION

The following are the different approaches I used to finding and maintaining a positive me.

Self-creation is not something that happens miraculously. It does not happen by accident but emanates from self-motivation. In finding yourself, you learn to create and maintain that harmonious lifestyle you seek. There are four main points that you should focus upon to help you harness that positive energy in becoming the best version of yourself.

CREATING A BALANCE

If you want a healthy relationship, you may need to first create balance in your own life. It's about addressing your own responsibilities before addressing someone else's. The balance perfects a a healthy life, by not being pulled in any one direction and not having too much of any one component. When your life and relationship are balanced, you have a sagacity of calm, motivation and a sense of clarity.

There are two main types of components to address when trying to balance one's life. Your internal and external elements. Often, we tend to put more emphasis on one element than the other, thus causing can imbalanced lifestyle.

Our internal element is made up of our inner feelings, guided by the heart and mind. This is where you place importance on self-reflection and soul searching. The internal element of your life is completely controlled by you, therefore, only you can address the concerns you have about yourself.

Sometimes, you find that some people spend so much of their time trying to focus on the internal element, that they forget to live and enjoy life. The external element, on the other hand, is how others see you and the way you do your daily activities. This is mainly steered by your physical and social life. A workaholic, for example, spends hours trying to get work done and rack up the numbers, he finds little time for his family and loved ones. People try and create a perfect external image of themselves, very often, as this is the part that others get to see firsthand.

Both elements are necessary in one's life, but don't over-exhaust yourself in trying to make it perfect. Creating balance within each element will help both aspects being fulfilled without overly accentuating and robbing your need of either. You will learn how to remain who you are and keep your man happy. It is important to look in your life to see which of these elements is being neglected and improve on it. Create a weekly list of tasks you need to fulfill and make a schedule for the time frame in which you want them completed. Keep a journal of all your accomplished goals and see which approach works best. Eventually, it will become routine, and you'll find that both your internal and external elements are aligned.

MEDITATION

"Between stimulus and response, there is a space. In that space is our power to choose our response."
~Viktor Frankl

IN THE hope of finding yourself, creating a balance and becoming Mrs Right, meditation plays an important role. This is the practice whereby techniques are used to focus and quieten the mind by achieving a higher level of inner calm and mental clarity. By meditating for some time each day, you enable yourself to handle stressful situations. Before you start your day, try this practice to allow the positive vibrations of life and the universe to flow through you. You cannot expect to receive positivity without expelling negativity.

GRATITUDE

I took Psychology as a major while studying at York University in Toronto. In my first semester, I remember learning about gratitude and how one could use it to change something negative with positivity. We were asked to present, over a thirty-days period, about something we were most grateful for in our lives. It is believed that by doing anything consistently over a period of 25 days, we can break old habits and create new ones. By applying the same principles to our relationship, we have the potential to rewire the brain into acknowledging and appreciating the blessings of our relationships.

Studies have shown that couples who apply these practices, lead longer, happier and healthier lives and also spark generosity in the others. Who wouldn't want that? As women, we sometimes have the tendency to blame our men about things not done, but neglect to say a simple 'thank you' for the things that they do. "Honey, thank you for taking out the trash last night," can leave a big impact with positive results.

I had the pleasure of sitting in at a couples' meeting a few months ago. Listening to couples having relationship issues and being at the brink of separation, some interesting examples were brought forth. They are of things we take for granted. One lady said she needed a separation from her husband because he was no longer working and therefore was unable to provide. I asked her about the other things he does. She said he helped with the kids and household chores. Why punish him for being down? Instead, she should have taken a different approach by showing gratitude for his help or even helped him find another job.

The goal as a couple is not to tear at each other but help build each other up. Life is guaranteed to take unexpected turns, and there is no point getting peeved about situations we cannot control. I know no one wants to live a poor, miserable and unhappy life, but you also made a vow (once you start a committed relationship) to stick with each other through the trying times.

'I love you' is a phrase often said out of habit, but with little to no real significance attached to it. Gratitude is not just about saying things because they sound nice, it is about sincerely meaning them. Gratitude is attitude. When I say 'I love you' to someone, I need to show the reasons why.

Women and men show, receive and expect love in different ways. For a woman, it is about complimenting her femininity. For a man, it's targeting his masculinity. A woman's sensitivity of love might be heightened by a gesture from her man — showering her with flowers or paying her a compliment about her beauty. As for a man, a feeling of empowerment and a boost of his ego might make him feel like a king. "Baby, I loved the way you took charge in that particular situation," topped with a dish of his favorite meal might be the gratuities he could relate to. By showing gratitude in our relationship, we are choosing to see the better side of our partners.

Over the course of the next month, you may want to begin a quest to show your partner 'gratitude'. Start by telling your man something new every day, a reason why you are grateful for having him. Top that by doing something to show him why. At first it might be easy, but after the first five days, you will begin to find it a little challenging. By sticking to this, however, you will be surprised to see how much your relationship will improve.

After my husband and I got married, we lived in separate countries for over a year. Every morning, when I woke up, I made it a point to show him how much he meant to me. Not only did it make us grow stronger as a couple, we also developed an irreplaceable and unbreakable bond of friendship that every relationship needs.

PART 8

PRINCIPLES OF LOVE

EVERY RELATIONSHIP will go through different stages and challenges of love. Some will sadly dissolve, while others will learn to accept their differences and work through the struggles to triumph. For a successful relationship, couples will need to become savvy by reading relationship books, observing other successful couples, attending couple's seminars, or simply browsing the internet. Regardless of the approach, there are principles to follow when trying to secure a successful relationship.

BE THERE FOR EACH OTHER

We all know that life is unpredictable and has a way of throwing curves at us. When the times get tough, couples will need to be a supporting pillar for each other. You will need to be there for each other and comfort and help the other heal and overcome whatever stressful times they are undergoing.

CHANGE THE WAY YOU DO THINGS

One of the biggest indicators of how things will turn out is the past. Doing things exactly as you did them will only yield the exact same results. Couples, who are successful, have learned that one must approach problems differently from the past in order to get a different result. Sometimes, the smallest change in the way we handle conflicts, make the biggest difference to the relationship.

ATTITUDE IS EVERYTHING

Your attitude plays a big role in your relationship. Immoral attitudes can bring about unscrupulous feelings and actions. It is important to change whatever bad attitudes you have developed towards each other.

CHANGE YOUR WAY OF THINKING

The way you and your partner view each other is very important. It affects how you perceive and expect things from the other. Be mindful of your expectations and learn to approach things practically. Life and people are imperfect. So, to seek perfection in someone is unwise.

STOP TRYING TO CHANGE EACH OTHER

Very often, when one enters a new relationship, they try to change the person to suit their own liking. One of the biggest mistakes you can make is to seek your happiness in someone else. Someone may be compatible with you and you may complement each other nicely but trying to change someone to fulfill your happiness is definitely not advisable.

The only person you can change is yourself. Once you learn to love and appreciate yourself, you will value and understand others better. Thus, creating the happiness you were searching for.

THE GRASS IS GREENER WHEN WATERED

Life is not like the romantic novels you read. There is no one coming to rescue you from your sorrows, so better learn to invest in your relationships and the things you want. You are the only one capable of making you and your relationship worthwhile. So, focus and work towards it.

YOU GET WHAT YOU GIVE

If you want love, time and understanding, then you must give love, time and understanding. The principle to karma is you reap what you sow.

CHANGE IS INEVITABLE

Changes in life and the things within are a constant. We use it to evolve, learn and grow. Don't hold on to things your spouse might have said or done in the past. We all go through different processes in life, and he might just not be at the same level of thinking as you are right now. Learn to be accommodating and patient.

PART 9

FORGIVENESS

ANYONE WHO is in a committed relationship will know that gratitude is closely related to forgiveness. When you begin a relationship, you open your heart to becoming emotionally vulnerable. No one is perfect and you will need to realise this sooner rather than later. Forgiveness and patience will always be needed in your relationship.

You may experience anger when your partner has wronged you but remembering the reason why you chose that person in the first place is important. I am not telling you to tolerate and condone abuse as that is a topic on a completely different scale. Choosing to forgive also gives you the chance to see how you may have contributed to the problem. If you are in a relationship, do not hold on to grudges or vengeance. Try not to bring up things that have occurred in the past. Equally, do not hold your partner captive and seek revenge for errors made. For a relationship to be successful, partners will have to show unrelenting patience and forgiveness. Know and acknowledge that your partner is human, therefore an imperfect person. If you are going to stay, learn to forgive and live peacefully. If not, forgive and let go.

The first step in forgiveness begins with learning to forgive yourself. Sometimes, we hold onto things done to us in the past and bring it forward. Learn to humbly admit your own faults and let them go. By choosing to forgive yourself, you are releasing inner pains and traumas while learning to let go off negative energies. You retain harmony and positive energies within yourself and in your relationship.

Allow yourself clarity of thought and empower yourself to rise above obstacles and pursue happiness. We have all seen women who are either afraid to enter a new relationship, or have done so, but brought with them all the hurt and pain from their past. They have setup this fence around their heart. You are denying yourself a chance to enjoy true love and cannot truly move on from disappointments if you cannot let go. When you let forgiveness in, you are allowing love to lead and ignite the way. This will bring peace and healing to your soul. It will set your heart and relationship free.

You may not realise, but when you hold on to the negative things in your life, you are creating a chain reaction for your children and their children, into thinking such is the norm of life. Someone might have hurt you in the past, this results in failure to trust your partner who has done nothing to you. So, you withhold the love and attention he deserves. You have children together and they grow up observing this. It will become a norm for them causing a domino effect which is passed on to future generations.

PART 10

WIN HIS MIND
TO WIN HIS HEART

THERE IS an old saying that the way to a man's heart is through his stomach. I say, the way to a man's heart, is through his mind. We have perfect housewives who are amazing cooks and house organisers, whom men leave in the hope of finding someone more driven and focused about life and success.

Sharing a life with someone who is committed and devoted are great traits to have when it comes to relationships and marriages. It is depicted in romance movies and stories told about love. These denote the idea of romantic love. Truth is people are not drawn together by coincidence or destiny. Social factors play an important role. People care about social stature of the person they are hoping to build a life with. If you look in society today, you might find that it is easier for a man to marry a woman who has had some form of post-secondary education than it is for him to do so with a less educated woman. He will factor in all the aspects of whether or not she is able to add something to the plate.

Think about it. If you were a man, and you had a chance to choose between a woman who is well domesticated and knows only that, and one who knows how to run her home, is driven, ambitious, challenges you and herself to do and be better, and manifests these actions in getting things done, who would you choose?

Trust me, if she is financially stable, she can pay to have someone else take care of the domestic duties. I asked a friend of mine recently, if he would leave a woman who he has been with for years, who takes care of the household, for someone who is more career based. His answer was indubitably yes! So, you see, many times you are killing yourself in the house trying to make him feel comfortable, when his interest is something else. Please be reminded that in most cases, even if he grows up in a single-parent home, it is more often with his mother. He would already know how to do all those household chores for himself.

Though there are many men who are confused about what type of a man they are, or those who just want to live a life filled with fun, and without any real commitment or significance, the greater percentage are, in fact, looking for that ideal lady to share life with. Men sometimes tell a partner that they are not ready to commit to a serious relationship, but truth be told, they are just not ready for a serious relationship with that particular person.

Men analyse women when they begin a relationship, and you may want to convince him that you can be a life-partner, before he makes his move. A man considers how you treat him, and he uses that to decide whether or not you will be a good life-long partner or mother to his children.

He searches for stability — in most cases financially and needs to know that you know how to deal with obstacles if they occur. His woman should be able to hold down the house should something happen to him. She should be able to direct the relationship towards a positive growth. Yes, there will be many obstacles, but he is depending on you as the partner to point the relationship in a positive direction.

You should not be at the same place you were in when you started the relationship years earlier. He needs a woman who makes him feel happy and with whom he can be himself. She should be able to make him laugh and is not too serious about life. Can keep him intrigued and on his toes.

Men love a woman who awe him and doesn't make life boring. He is looking for a woman he sees a way to grow with and knows that in any situation she will have his back. She should be able to make choices without having to depend solely on his decisions.

THE GOOD STUFF

Sex is all important in a relationship and is one of the fundamentals in winning a man's mind. It is more so about the quality of sex, than it is about the activity itself. I'm not telling you to become gymnasts or to sign up for pole dancing classes, though I'm sure he wouldn't mind that. Sex isn't just about rubbing private parts together, but rather about being able to experience all the pleasures and allowing someone into the depths of your soul through the ultimate satisfaction in the art of love-making. Men need sex in their relationship to function well. It is a part of their genetic makeup. It is your duty, as his woman, to fulfill that need, likewise him to you. Any man, who is sexually satisfied, is a happy man.

Any pattern of activity which is repeated frequently, becomes boring over time. By incorporating new and exciting things into your sex life, not only will you blow his mind, and increase sexual satisfaction, you will also help him eliminate building sexual interest in someone else. It has been proven, that sex also helps in improving insomnia and lethargic behaviours, by increasing the mental and physical state of mind. So, the next time you see your once grumpy co-worker in a happy mood, it might just be the result of a good love-making session.

Share with each other your sexual fantasies. Some of you might be too embarrassed to do so, but if someone is right for you, sharing your deepest fantasies should not be an issue as it is the responsibility of both in making sure you are sexually satisfied. How will you know his desires if none of you are willing to talk about it? I do agree that some fetishes can be a little too exciting, but who knows? He might just turn out to be a bigger freak than you are. Make sex fun! Talk to each other during sex and tell him things you'd like done to you. One thing I like doing during sex is playing sex games, which tells you different positions to try and different places to do them.

A man loves an attractive woman, dress up for him. Buy nice lingerie and give him a little surprise now and again. For some guys, it's wearing costumes, maybe a nurse or a maid? Smell good for your man. Guys find good fragrances a huge turn on, he will find you irresistible and it will make him just want to eat you right up.

As outrageous as this might sound, it is true! I have met so many women who didn't even know it was possible for a female to have an orgasm. Crazy, right? You'd be surprised to find out that there are many couples who are so routine and who just have sex for the sake of having sex. When having sex with Mr Right, it should be so much fun that your knees shake, eyes roll, you reach for the heavens, sing hallelujah and scream his name.

I know, it is difficult to identify a man who is right for you. There are some men who are very pretentious and make you believe that they have all the bells and whistles you seek in your Mr Right.

They do everything in their power to win you over and once they get what they want, they are M.I.A. I've learned over the years that time is valuable, and all is revealed with the passage of time. That is why it is important to go through dating stages to learn more about someone you are hoping to share life with. Sex should only be shared between people who are right for each other. I say this because it is a sacred activity that allows someone into your hallowed temple. Sex takes you to another dimension where only someone special should be allowed to venture through those realms with you.

It is important that one observes sexual faithfulness in their relationship. Having devoted yourself to someone and with whom you have a desire to share life, you open yourself to him: your senses, mind, body, heart and soul. When you compromise that devotion with other people, you sacrifice the sexual faithfulness you have built with your spouse.

Protect that sacredness with everything you have and bestow it entirely and completely on your partner. Be conscious of the consequences of not practising self-discipline. We live in a world where we are tempted every day but focus on your relationship and do not allow things to destroy your sexual faithfulness to your partner. The happiness and trust in your relationship will depend on it.

PRIVACY IN THE RELATIONSHIP

Privacy is a very important factor in your relationship. People can know of your relationship without knowing about it. Many times, issues will arise between your partner and you. Your first response may be to call up a friend or family member to tell them or seek their advice. Though it is good that you have people who love and care about you, who provide a strong support system, you should be mindful of where you seek counsel, as not everyone should be allowed to interfere in your life and the choices you make within your relationship.

When you seek advice from your family and friends, it is important to remember that they are your family and your friends. Your loved ones may make judgements and decisions on your behalf. They will tell you things they know you want to hear at that particular time, which could end up being more damaging or by increasing pressure resulting in making irrational decisions.

When you make your own choices in your relationship, you are not entertaining the negative ideas of others to impair your judgments and are making choices based on your own understanding of your relationship.

At the end of the day when all is said and done and you have forgiven and forgotten whatever diminutive problems there were between your partner and you, your family and friends will always remember the ugly image that you conjured up for them during that stressful time.

They will forever resent him and make judgments based on trivial issues as an injustice to you. By handling your own glitches with your man, it will strengthen your bond and help you to gain more respect for each other.

SOCIAL MEDIA

Social media has become an important part of our daily lives. It helps us connect with friends, family, long-lost loved ones and the rest of the world. However, with its increased fame and popularity, couples become eager to showcase their everyday activities of the good, the bad and the indifference.

For maintaining a happy and healthy relationship, you must realize that privacy is prudent. Being private does not mean being secretive about your life but being careful about how much personal information you divulge to the public. Whatever happens behind closed doors is for you and your partner to know. Social media is not a reality television show, nor is it a therapist's office. Truth be told, half of your contacts do not care about what happens in your life, and the other half are just praying for the moment you slip up to make a mockery of you. Many women use the platform of social media to honor and praise their men, only to discriminate and condemn them days later. This behaviour makes you look cheap and petite. It proves the reason why he cannot commit to you.

PART 11

STOP GIVING BOYFRIENDS
THE 'HUSBAND PRIVILEGES'

IN A previous chapter, I had mentioned that a woman should act like a wife even before she becomes one.

Some women are stuck in relationships (girlfriend position) for five or 10 years, some even longer, with a man who does not show any clear sign of what his true intentions about commitment are. To be honest, I do not believe that a man needs half a decade to know if you are right for him. I am sure you have heard the saying so many times, "If he knows, he knows."

Often, we have seen women investing their years, time, and energy in the wrong man, only for him to find a new person and marry her in less than no time. Many women sacrifice their youth and fidelity, giving up education, careers, and a trustworthy and meaningful life for a man who will only use her without the intention of ever making her a wife.

It is time for women to wise up and stop giving such men the power to use them. Why should you sell yourself short or continue to invest yourself in a relationship not knowing if he will ever commit?

It does not matter how long you have been going out with him, dated him, have lived with him, how many children you have with him, if there is no legal binding before God and the law. The man is not your husband until you have a valid marriage certificate to show. He is only your boyfriend.

I do not think it is right for a woman to invest multiple years in a man, bear his children and be a perfect housewife and give him the best possible treatment, only to have to beg him to marry or fully commit to her. He wants to have his cake and eat it too. There was a time when living together before marriage was considered highly immoral. Today, the scenario is very different. It now is the norm to be living together before marriage.

A research conducted by the National Center for Family and Marriage Research, where data was collected between 1974 and 1995, showed that only 11% of women lived with their significant other before marriage. However, from 2010 to 2013 there was a major increase to 69%.

Understandably, the times have changed and couples are trying to figure out if they can coexist with each other before they decide to take the ultimate leap. But is this really wise? Think about this too. If you are a man who gets sex whenever you desire, come home to a hot meal at the end of the day, have someone to wash your dirty clothes, take care of your children and clean the house, why would you ever really want to get married? You already have someone playing the role of your wife and doing all the things you need without you having to marry her.

And you being that girlfriend, your dreams that he will see your hard work and hopes that he sees your value will all be broken. Your actions have sadly trapped you into just being the girlfriend. Playing house does not compensate for a marriage. Until you realize that you are worth much more than the choices you make, it will never change. Marriage is a lifelong commitment, a promise, a sacred covenant to each other that you want to spend life with that person. It is about working together even when the times get hard. Living as partners gives room to just bail out without really trying to work through the hardships. There is no commitment and really nothing there to make you want to be together. In other words, it is the easy way out.

Due to this, one may find it difficult to handle issues in the future as you never really took the time to try and resolve these issues. This may affect future relationships, leading to further separations. I will stress this point again from a previous chapter, that it is imperative for couples to court and date before becoming intimate. This will help to know your compatibilities with the person you are hoping to share your life with.

In addition to this, women sometimes think that having a child will make him stay. This, my dears, is far from the truth. A baby does not make your boyfriend a husband, it makes him a father, a parent. This is one of the many reasons why we have so many baby-mother dramas. Some women use a child to trap a man and force him to commit. It is even worse to get pregnant for a man who is not ready to be a father. You may think that he will have to take care of his child so you will always have him around. Before you know it, you end up being a single mother with the man not caring at all about the child.

Sometimes, we make decisions solemnly based on our own emotions that can cause a lot more pain and heartache in the end. You will need to ask yourself the difficult questions like will he ever consider having you as a wife, will he be there for me and our child should I get pregnant, will he be good to us? If you have even an ounce of doubt about this and cannot answer loudly and proudly, then I think you know the real answers to your questions.

Consider should something happen to a man you have devoted your life to. You will not be a beneficiary to any life insurances, you would not be included in any retirement funds, bank accounts or any monitory funding. You will just end up being left high and dry. Boyfriends and husbands are two separate classes. Your boyfriend might be generous to you and may have given you gifts and such, but a girlfriend does not share the same privileges as a wife.

When you marry, you build a trust by making financial decisions together. You make big financial purchases like houses and cars. It would be much harder to invest in someone you are not fully committed to. You will hesitate to co-sign for big purchases, as you may question the possibility of a break-up. There is a certainty that as a girlfriend you will not be given access to many of the things I just mentioned.

Happiness and morals, or even the opportunity of finding someone who will actually love you should not be compromised by getting stuck with someone who will not sacrifice anything for you. You are worth a lot more than that and deserve the very best. If a man truly loves you, there will be no doubt in his mind that you are the one for him and the person he wants to build and share his life's journey with.

Acknowledgements

Let me begin by acknowledging you, my dear readers. Thank you for opening to the possibility of welcoming change in your life and the candidness to see things from a different perspective. By doing so you are helping to create a 'you' that you want for yourself. A person who is aware and confident about knowing her own and other's expectations.

I extend a warm thank you to the team who worked hard in making this book a possibility. My publisher and editor Kaberi Dutta Chatterjee, my editor, Priti Raghavan, and graphic designer, Anirban Paul. I am thankful to my family and friends for helping to spread the word and sharing this book with others. Finally, a big thank you to my darling husband who was there to support the crazy dream of putting my thoughts into words.

I love you.

About the Author

Cedella Blanchard was born and raised in St Catherine, Jamaica. In 2007, at the age of 20, she immigrated to Canada with her family to pursue better opportunities. Today, Cedella is a wife and mother. She also studies Psychology at York University in Toronto and works as a Pharmacy Technician.

She wrote the book **Why Men Run away** to empower women all over the world who are faced with fairy-tale expectations of love and long-term relationships. You will find that there is no such thing as a perfect love story and every relationship, even the happiest ones, come with their fair share of struggles. However, it is not about the conflicts or differences you will face, but rather the approach that helps to resolve them.

Leave these pages with a clear vision and perspective of how you want to view love.

6
0B/1804